The Scabbard of Her Throat

The Scabbard of Her Throat

Bernadette Geyer

THE WORD WORKS
Hilary Tham Capital Collection
WASHINGTON, D.C.

FIRST EDITION   FIRST PRINTING
The Scabbard of Her Throat
Copyright © 2013 by Bernadette Geyer

Reproduction of any part of this book in any form or by any means, electronic or mechanical, including photocopying, must be with permission in writing from the publisher. Address inquiries to:

The WORD WORKS
PO Box 42164
Washington, DC 20015

wordworksbooks.org

editor@wordworksbooks.org

Cover art: "Like Taking the Black off a Crow," mixed-media collage by Kathleen Kendall.

Author photo by Veralana Photography.
Book design by Janice Olson.

Library of Congress Control Number: 2012950825
International Standard Book Number: 978-0-915380-85-5

Acknowledgments

Poems from this book have appeared or are forthcoming in the following publications, sometimes in a modified version:

32 Poems: "Thumbelina's Mother Speaks: To Thumbelina" and "Thumbelina's Mother Speaks: To the Toad's Mother"; *Atticus Review*: "The Space She Leaves"; *Barn Owl Review*: "The Sword Swallower Finds a New Calling"; *Beltway Poetry Quarterly*: "I Become Like Proust" and "Three Birds"; *Center: A Journal of the Literary Arts*: "Without Warning"; *Crab Creek Review*: "Dressing the Naked Sushi Model"; *Dislocate*: "Just So"; *Dos Passos Review*: "A Matter of Principle"; *Ellipsis*: "Echo"; *Flyway*: "I Become Like Proust"; *Hotel Amerika*: "Three Birds"; *Innisfree Poetry Journal*: "My Mother's Thumbs"; *The Marlboro Review*: "The Door"; *The Midwest Quarterly*: "Seamstress"; *No Tell Motel*: "Egg, Potato, Stone" and "Oyster Shells"; *North American Review*: "Odds"; *The Oxford American*: "I Believe"; *roger: an art & literary magazine*: "Carousel"; *Verse Daily*: "Without Warning"; *Waccamaw*: "Pit"; *Weave*: "That Winter."

"Gift" appeared in the anthology *Poetic Voices without Borders*, by Gival Press. "The Door" was reprinted in *Poetic Voices without Borders, 2nd Edition*, by Gival Press.

I would like to thank the Arts Council of Fairfax County for a Strauss Fellowship, which supported the development of this manuscript. I am grateful for the love and support of my family and the encouragement and valuable feedback of my friends, especially Cynthia Marie Hoffman, Deborah Ager, Reb Livingston, Sally Rosen Kindred, Julie Brooks Barbour, Angela Vogel, Renee Soto, Sandra Beasley, and Luke Johnson. I would also like to thank Cornelius Eady and The Word Works' Nancy White, Karren Alenier, and Janice Olson for bringing this book into the world.

For Peter and Frida

Contents

1.

Thumbelina's Mother Speaks: *To Thumbelina*   ~11
Heat   ~12
After Having Been Distracted   ~13
Carousel   ~15
He Was   ~16
Without Warning   ~17
Afternoon on Portland Harbor   ~18
I Believe   ~20
Gift   ~21
Daughter   ~22
Another Miracle   ~24

2.

Thumbelina's Mother Speaks: *To the Witch*   ~27
Echo   ~28
That Winter   ~30
Odds   ~31
Three Birds   ~32
The Spider   ~33
The Thimble   ~35
The Illusion All Along   ~36
Women I Could Have Been   ~38

3.

Thumbelina's Mother Speaks: *To the Toad's Mother* ~43
The Door ~44
Of Widowhood ~45
The Sword Swallower Finds a New Calling ~46
Afterwards ~47
The Space She Leaves ~48
New Porch ~49
My Mother's Thumbs ~50
I Become Like Proust ~51
Dressing the Naked Sushi Model ~53
Egg, Potato, Stone ~54
At a Distance ~55
Pit ~56

4.

Thumbelina's Mother Speaks:
   To Hans Christian Andersen ~59
Asthma Attack ~60
Diorama of a Grand Failure ~61
Just So ~62
My Mother's Tongue ~63
Nature Center ~64
Oyster Shells ~65
Bath ~66
A Matter of Principle ~67
Seamstress ~68
Advice to My Daughter
   Regarding Houses in the Woods ~69

About the Author / About the Artist ~72
About the Hillary Tham Capital Collection ~73
About The Word Works ~74

1

THUMBELINA'S MOTHER SPEAKS

~ To Thumbelina

How many nights I knelt befouled by stars
in that garden, yet my belly still refused
to swell. No husband—just this body.
Not even knowledge of the ways of men.
I don't recall the color of the seed,
that witch-gift planted by my anxious hands.
And little does it matter now the color
of that bloom. You were my blossom-born,
emerging from a womb that wasn't mine.
As soon as I inhaled your pollen-scented
hair, I understood that I would lose you:
all children are but born to leave.
Not once did I hear you call me Mother.
Know this: after you I never sought another.

HEAT

In summer's heat, I'd wet a handkerchief and spread
it across my back as the oscillating fan marked time
in the distance between headboard and footboard:
the nightly sentry that made sleep possible in that house
where we struggled to simply shift the burdensome air.
No matter how stifling, that damp cotton square and the fan's
steady breaths allowed my body to forget the heat
long enough for sleep's broom to scatter the dust
of my consciousness. The fan's hum stole into my dreams—
a motorboat one night, a hive the next. Steady drone.
White noise of my youth. Some nights it was enough
to make me shiver, my body goosepimpled and naked.
How reckless and naïve in my sleep—windows open,
and all that night air with nowhere to go.

AFTER HAVING BEEN DISTRACTED

If not for the singular cicada trill,
I'd have continued the August afternoon,
head swimming in the fictions
of the book on my lap,
legs propped on the porch railing.

But that staccato drew my focus
to a wasp, clasped to the cicada's back,
riding those wings blurred
with the struggle to escape,
to lift their bearer—like Lazarus—
out from the premature welcome
of an earthen embrace.

The trill stuttered, then stopped.
Minutes passed before two weak notes
again trembled upward: the cicada still alive
in the unbelievable way a man can emerge—
pie-eyed and smoke-dark—
from the engulfed apartment he awoke to.

I searched out the cicada, saw on its back
a soft pink crater, a trail of ants already forming.
The cicada flipped to expose a belly
of twitching legs as my own steady fingers
curled around a fist-sized rock.
A short last note escaped its body
as I struck with the stone
again and again until the cicada's legs stilled.

The background noise of life
retuned in increments to the yard—
a twitter, a rustling—
as a swell of godlike benevolence
churned inside me.

CAROUSEL

      Fevered, we ride.
Mad mouths in pursuit:
      lips drawn,
teeth bared at the bit.

      Our world defined
by a crude circumference,
      in turn both
pursuer and pursued.

HE WAS

longer than my index finger, pale hairs
bristled out, yellow spires at his neck
which bobbed as he crept onto the curved
bark I held as a ship to ferry him from
the dangerous shore beneath my daughter's slide
to the safety of the north side
of the northernmost tree in the stand of pines
in our backyard. Placing him where we thought
he'd be most out-of-the-way, we carried on
as elves picking pine cones for Santa's reindeer.
Every few minutes, she'd run to see
what the caterpillar was up to. *He's on the tree.
Okay. Leave him alone.* But we are born
not knowing when or how to leave things be,
our hands emerging clutched around something
we spend entire lives learning how to let go.
Then, her running around the tree, panting
Mommy, I don't see him anymore. His body
now half-curled and writhing at the tree's base
in a depression in the mulch so slight
it could've been made by a child's foot.
And while a part of me wanted to say *Now look
what you've done! I told you to leave him alone,*
I simply told her he needed to be alone
because he was trying to sleep and anyway
it was time for us to go inside and start dinner.
But by the way we both sighed at the clumsiness
of our own best intentions, I think she knew.

WITHOUT WARNING

No one ever warns how low
clouds can bend to lap the bay
with thirsty, gossamer tongues.

Or how life is consistently reduced
to forms of water, returning to puddles
and tears, rivers and sweat.

They don't mention how quickly
a storm can gather and cross the bay
in the rushed flight of wings and sails.

Or that life can end like this:
the fishy smell of the shore builds
and sours in your stomach, the language

of the living replaced by *swish* and *thrum*.
Nature's incongruous voices
will fail to disclose that your last breath
                              may be used to laugh.

AFTERNOON ON PORTLAND HARBOR

The Bagheera Schooner drifts—two sails up,
two to go—and we become part of the harbor vista.

Other tour boats pass us; their passengers
wave, take pictures. Our crew

hoists the remaining sails, working
aft to fore while we sit back, let the wind run

across the decks of our bodies. Sun
dipping in and out of sight as the jib

bobs against the horizon. Slowly tacking
port to starboard, our bow passes

through the eye of the wind; we head away
from shore in a close hauled point of sail. As we near

the old fort, the crew loosens the ropes, tacks
the sails, tightens the ropes again.

They demonstrate: lean, pull, take up the slack,
repeat. Double half hitch to hold it tight.

A sudden wind shift slaps the sails; the boat heels
to starboard. We prostrate ourselves,

perpendicular to the water, not knowing
whether what we feel against our faces

is the true wind or the apparent. Gravity tugs
us along the tilted deck—our braced thighs hum

to the heartbeat of keel against water.
The crew feathers the sails to lessen the heel.

Hush the harbor soothes as we slow
to a near-stall. Buoy bells toll

the passage of wind and time. We allow
ourselves to be carried away

by both. Bow into the eye of the wind,
our wake broadens behind us.

I BELIEVE

~ for Tammy Faye, 1942-2007

The longer I live, the less I believe
in the singular rightness
of what I have chosen to believe.

And I've begun
to believe in the rightness of belief,
in general.

I've begun to believe that, maybe,
I've been wrong
all along about Chaucer's Pardoner,

his bags of stones
and sheep-bone relics. Maybe,
sometimes, the ends

do justify the means, and every falseness
has its moment—
however brief—of sacred truth.

Then again, maybe belief
in a "prosperity gospel" is simply easier
than belief in nothing.

So pardon me
as I gather my precious bones
into this bag

I call *body*. These penance-worn rags
no relics. And me?
No saint anyone should believe in.

GIFT

> ~ *after the sculpture "Gift 3" by Barbara Liotta*

He gave her a gift
of stones.
Hefty, weighted
with the love
of a whole history
of earth.
Solid, smooth,
pocked with age.
Each stone
she collected like years,
the years
she collected like gifts,
each holding her feet
to earth, holding
earth to her feet.
Dimpled, marbled,
timeless.
Solid, smooth,
pregnant with meaning.
He gave her meaning,
a gift of stones.

DAUGHTER

For weeks, your name scrawled itself
across canvases in art galleries,
narrated to us from the VH1 pop band
documentaries that sucked away hours
of the last child-free evenings
your father and I had together.
Even cartoons punch-lined your name,
morphed images of that lush-browed painter
in hilariously impossible situations
until, finally, that name broke through
the thinned bubble of ignorance
we'd blown around ourselves.
We let your name in. Of course!—How
could we not have recognized it?

~

All those you could have been.
All those you would take for yourself.
But we wrote it first. And we wrote it official.
No matter what you would have us call you.
No matter how many stories
in which you call yourself by another name.
In which you call yourself Emily, Rose,
or Invisible Erica, as if names were accessories
swapped out depending on your mood,
fast and simple as changing Barbie's shoes.
But the hours your father and I scrawled
away, the myriad hours, myriad names,

all your potential futures like the daydreamed
Mrs. Crush-boy scribbled over and over
on the cover of a high school notebook.
No you cannot so easily swap it for another.
We have proof. See here. This paper.
By which we mean to say: you are ours.

ANOTHER MIRACLE

Mad God has water in his hands,
my daughter says, *and he spills it*

all over the street. Her Noah's Ark
floats on linoleum and the animals

swim. We play flood all morning
as hills of snow thaw outside.

On Christmas Eve, we pilgrimage
to the remote land of the Craft Room,

retrieve Mary, Joseph, and Baby Jesus
from the displaced safety of the ark.

Desert sand transforms to Berber
and we descend arid mountains

as if they were mere flights of stairs.
Everywhere I look, another miracle

is happening. In her hands, the wise men
on their camels are taking flight.

2

THUMBELINA'S MOTHER SPEAKS

~ *To the Witch*

I didn't come to hear you parse your words
like gnat hairs for a spell. I came to say
that you are nothing but an old woman:
gnarled bones and parchment skin do not make you
a witch. No special powers come with warts.
Your stoop—no sign of other-worldly wisdom:
time's constant breath bends us the way
that coastal trees are shaped against their will.
How many were there, tricked into belief
that tender lives could grow from sterile seeds
and thrive in soil worked by sorrow's hands?
Like Eve, we were beguiled to know beyond
the bastion of our naïve garden's wall.
So high the ladders we built, only to fall.

ECHO

It's like she said *Here, have some pain,*
and when I adjusted to that she said *Here*

have some more, ratcheting up
the transducer's pressure against my chest

to find not just my heart, but each valve—
mitral, tricuspid, pulmonary and aortic.

At night, I have heard the misfire,
the subtle sucking back one chamber makes,

unwilling to let everything swim away from it.
Then she said *I have to press harder here,*

trick it into seeing between your ribs.
And now I envy Adam his stolen rib, his lack of breasts.

The nurse says *Don't breathe so deeply*
and I am surprised to be breathing at all.

I pant like a dog to keep my lungs out of the way,
as she presses my breast aside. The heart's valves

echo, reply. I want to tell her *NO, my heart*
is not so hidden; look here and here,

but still the pressing continues.
My heart remains merely a ghost

to the transducer's sonar that pings
the cavity of my thorax. What good

is a four-chambered heart—this hornets' nest
of blood and faulty valves? Its complexity

masks its fragility. This nurse, does she
consider herself a detective? an explorer? the Cold War

intelligentsia? Her hand lifts: I suck air
deep into my lungs, which buoy me up

above the pain as I notice my clenched fist
against my face, a numbing in my tensed left hip.

Even with its redundancies, the four-chambered heart
is inadequate. Its prolapse sucks the departing blood

back into its chambers, like when you embrace
someone in farewell but secretly snip a lock of their hair.

The nurse rolls me a little towards her and says
Now for your abdominal artery, I will look through

your stomach, lowering her hand again onto my body.
I have forgotten how to move on my own.

THAT WINTER

His name was a lozenge on her tongue,
diminished by what saliva she could muster.
Heady with their confessions to each other,
they got drunk on just the thought of getting drunk.

They cut rancid meat from the bone
and boiled the bone for soup,
watered down the remnants of the broth
and sipped the weak tea.

They shared the buried treasure
of the last onion, and when their pantry
yawned its empty maw, they feasted
on words, syllables salting their tongues.

A thick roux of memories, savored—
vowels like raw yolks she feared
would break in their mouths.
The long O of hope spread thin on a crust.

ODDS

Eighty percent of all plane crashes occur in the first
three minutes or in the last minute of the flight.

The odds of winning the lottery are 1 in 18 million
but you can't win if you don't play. In Peru,

between 2004 and 2007, 4 out of 10 murdered women
were killed by their husband or boyfriend.

The chances of being injured are greatest in your own
home. If you are driving in your car and you see

two cars crash into each other up ahead, you should
drive toward the exact point where those cars crashed.

Odds are they will be elsewhere when you get there.
This is called "driving into the accident."

The doctor tells you he diagnosed you early, so your odds
of survival are good. Very good. But then you cross

the street, get in your car and drive home to the step stool
with its wobbly leg. The box of good china on the high

shelf in the closet. Your lover, who welcomes you home
with a kiss. All the knives in the kitchen.

THREE BIRDS

Three birds
drifted to the ground
like leaves.

As I drew nearer,
I realized they were
leaves.

No matter how far
I walked away from
those leaves,

never again
could they be
three birds.

THE SPIDER

I noticed the spider
      just as we began
           to make love, and

at first my eyes kept
      moving from your chin
           past your shoulder

up to where the spider
      scuttled along the
           crown molding

(how slow
      your movements,
           how fast his) as if

he knew he had
      intruded, as if to
           quickly leave us to

it. Then for a while
      it was easy to forget
           him, you above me—

our bodies
      joined and eight-
           appendaged.

But when we'd
      finished I looked up
           to see him now on

 the wall opposite
   our bed. And
      after our breathing

had begun to
   slow, I—
      vulnerable and

naked—asked you
   to kill him.
      And you did.

THE THIMBLE

Of all the things I've used
        to drain the ocean,
                I love the thimble best,

how it magnifies the task
        beyond all sense of futility.
                No bucket or barge,

no syringe or sink
        for me—just the thimble,
                with its pocked hood,

its fluted lip. Dip by dip,
        my goal a surge
                as near as it will ever be.

THE ILLUSION ALL ALONG

Summer. Scent of honeysuckle. Danger
of feasting bees. I'd finally had enough
of those Landfair siblings, who swarmed
my neighborhood like a plague
of white trash locusts. Who wouldn't
have wanted to play on our swing set,
so near the edge of our yard's steep slope
each pump and thrust cantilevered our legs out
over dangerous heights?

That day, when their youngest daughter appeared
in the yard, I stomped to my bedroom, where I sat
with my reflection in the window until I saw
her cross the street back to her house.
My proud legs carried me down the stairs,
into the kitchen, where a chair leg
tripped me, sent me face first into the corner
of the wooden door, propped open to let in air.

Dazed, I stumbled. Blood dripped
onto the floor. Then, wet paper towels.
Confusion. Butterfly bandages.
The station wagon's front seat. Cold hands
on me in the emergency room. Hands held me
down, strapped me to a hospital bed.

The metallic taste of blood seeped down
the back of my throat. *Do you want to watch?*
I refused the offered mirror, would ever after
learn to make peace with the visible scar.
Up close hands on my face. Needle

passed left to right. The thread
surprisingly resembled any other thread.
When they were done, a gauze patch
like a fist under my nose.

After that: the forgetting that lifted the pain
the way a magician's hand lifts
his unremarkable handkerchief
to reveal an empty cage and we realize
the dove had been the illusion all along.

WOMEN I COULD HAVE BEEN

One with eyes
full of self-immolation.

One with buckling knees
on legs that forgot how to run
through open fields.

One with fingers
scarred from biting, hands
adorned with the tics
of her neurosis.

One whose words
do not match her thoughts.
One whose tongue won't flick
the words from her throat.

One with too many words
cluttering her mouth.
One whose words
are dictated by others.

One whose faith
was stolen by thieves.

One whose body folds
into itself with age.
One whose gnarled hands
conjure ghosts.

One whose callused fingertips
pluck life into taut strings,
remembering the one
who taught her to play.

The forsaken one. The chosen.

3

THUMBELINA'S MOTHER SPEAKS

~ *To the Toad's Mother*

With each year's passing, grief dilutes itself
within my body, portioned out the way
a flash flood ultimately finds a meek
abode to welcome every soiled drop.
In letting go, I learned to be a "good"
mother, the kind who disciplines herself
to think only of what's best for her child.
Of course, that's why you seized *her* for your son—
deluded as you were to think she'd stay.
The sky is never bluer than we dare
imagine it to be. As we think
then so it is. At times, I understand
the desperate hands that reach for more—
and yet, I kick the cat who scratches at my door.

THE DOOR

The door is immeasurable.

The door opens or closes; it is all the same to her. The door is still a door.

The door prevents her from hearing the pissy trickle of the water fountain in the courtyard. Tossing coins is forbidden.

The door moves, gives slightly beneath her slick, desperate palms; it jiggles in its frame, loose as a body beneath its clothes.

He is on the other side of the door.

The door is just a door. Only when she wakes and washes the night from her skin can she understand this.

The door is painted yellow, the color of abandonment, to match the ribbons in her front yard (in the branches of her hair, binding her limbs, her torso).

Perhaps he will always be on the other side of the door.

How to sum up the nature of a door—if one passes through it often enough, it becomes irrelevant.

OF WIDOWHOOD

She had no pockets—my father's mother—only
sleeves that collared her wrists even in summer.
In the church pew, like a magician, she'd wriggle
from the starched cuff of her sleeve a handkerchief,
the small gift of it unwrapped to reveal a housekey,
two peppermint candies, and a dollar for the collection basket.
Lipstick? That was applied at home. No need for
the purse full of items I, at ten, thought a lady should carry.
But what did I know, back then, of widowhood?
With every frown that puckered her lips when the man
in the pew behind us burst into song, I learned that it is better
to bear the hymns with a still tongue than to pierce
the ears of the faithful by singing proudly off-key.

THE SWORD SWALLOWER FINDS A NEW CALLING

She swallows stones, now—
throat like a creek bed.
Started with pebbles. Palmed
several to warm them
before she plucked one,
placed it in her mouth,
tongued its smooth surface, imagined it
transubstantiated into a pearl.

She filled herself with pearls
until her skin rivaled their milkiness.
Under the floodlights, she glowed,
audiences rapt as they never had been
when it was just another trick,
sword seeming to disappear
in the scabbard of her throat.

She savored another stone,
tasted the vinegary remnants
of a thousand compressed years.
She felt a kinship
with the grain of sand she imagined
locked within the stone's heart,
which could have begun life
in the mouth of another creature,
could have evolved
into something else entirely.

AFTERWARDS

She lost hers first. And I
was the first to learn, sitting cross-legged
    on the floor of her dorm room,
the pot of Earl Grey steaming

    between us because this was not
an occasion for underage libation
    but one that called for clarity
of mind. We spoke not about how

    it felt, but about how it felt
afterwards—after the endorphins
    faded. Not about the act itself,
but what having done it meant.

    In truth, we probably didn't speak
to each other much at all. The tea
    cooled and the snow fell outside
the window and we put on our best

    solemn grownup faces and were moved
by the thought of being moved by it all.
    Stilled by the crush of importance
of even the act of lifting our cups

    from their saucers to our girlish lips.
We sipped the bitterness that comes
    with steeping, looked at each other,
and then looked away.

THE SPACE SHE LEAVES

> ~ *after the photo "The Tuileries Gardens, 1980"*
> *by André Kertész*

The chair's shadow leans against a stone
column in the foreground of the photo. Metal

flakes from the chair's round rusted seat.
With curved arms frail as sandpiper legs,

it gestures the feeble welcome it has
extended for decades. In the background,

a young girl—black wool coat tented
above stockings pulled knee-high—

bounds away from the dark pant leg
of her mother, whose body straddles

the worlds existing within and without
the photo's margins. The chair seems

to watch them as it suns itself, basking
in Tuileries Gardens on a day that could be

any other day, but isn't. On this day
a young girl runs from her mother,

tests the freedom that comes with distance,
looks back to watch what fills the space

she leaves behind. On this day, a mother
straddles two worlds for her daughter,

who cannot see the woman, caught
by a camera's lens, turning away.

NEW PORCH

The porch—its chipped paint peeling—is a poor
replacement for the yard my sister left
behind. She opens up the door to let

her beagle sniff the summer air. On Leap
Day—just six months ago—she would have called
you crazy had you told her she'd be so

content. She says it's just on garbage day
the noise of alley-facing windows gets
to her. Our parents say the porch will need

to be redone before the winter comes.
For now, it waits as she ignores the phone,
ignores the mail. The lawyer sent the forms

for her to sign. *It seems so final, and
too difficult to think about.* I tell
her not as difficult as packing up

a house one afternoon while he's at work.
A grace of wind blows through the screen. She says
We'll have to blast that porch to strip it clean.

MY MOTHER'S THUMBS

Picked raw by nervous fingernails,
my mother's thumbs are scarred
and always bleeding. She has worried

her way through cartons of bandages
and gauze over her three daughters,
her husband. When I was a child,

I believed my mother could quash
Satan himself, like a gnat, under
her great ragged and powerful

thumbs. But now, I grasp her hands
in mine across the kitchen table
as we talk, thinking I am saving

those coarse digits, if only
for a moment. Instead, I merely
delay the inevitable movements,

talismans that keep her family safe.
Women in churches finger rosaries,
whispering prayers, but I

have learned to put my faith
in scabs that nervous hands
will not allow to heal.

I BECOME LIKE PROUST

It is now twenty years
that we have been meeting like this,
in out-of-the-way diners
where we are sure to go unrecognized.

Twenty years, and I no longer know
what to say to you—the mystery
long gone like the color in your beard,
the tautness of my figure.

You'd think I'd have grown more comfortable
with these long silences but
instead I become like Proust,
noticing how you lay out your cutlery—

parallel, equidistant.
I note each fray in the cuff
of your sleeve; which buttons
have recently been restitched

with a thread slightly whiter than
the rest. I listen to each syllable
uttered at the table next to us,
allowing diphthong and syntax

to roll around my head the way you
play wine against your tongue
before you swallow. How I hate
seeing you through this microscope

that I have taken to carrying—your
imperfections magnified until they
edge you out of the picture, distort
memory, chase me away one more time.

DRESSING THE NAKED SUSHI MODEL

When she lays her body on the stage in front of you,
    ignore how her breasts, though small, lean

one to each side of her torso. Layer the nests
    of shredded radish as if her skin were bark

and she the last tree at the end of the world,
    the last hope of the future's mythic birds

who will recount the honor consigned
    for her stillness as you set one roll after another

along her sternum, hiding the scar whose flesh
    would never tan. Your art dwells as much

in the heed and the hand's hovering,
    as in the final impression you create.

Shave carrots to spine the ebi dragon,
    stalled on its way from her clavicle

to the rawest parts of her. Slice the lemon
    so thin that if held to the eye you could discern

the tart angles of everything. When finished,
    rise and bow as the spectators gather,

chopsticks poised, remarking how one pale flesh
    can be indistinguishable from another.

EGG, POTATO, STONE

In the photo, ten of them.
Mottled, trailing bracken, huddled
on a parched, cracked backdrop
gray as when the indecisive sky

changes with each blink: now
shades of *winter-before-snowfall*,
now *dawn-following-the-illness*.
They could be anything. Flat

landscape of a blank doll face.
Emotionally cryptic as a clown.
If they are eggs, they are not
mine. They are eggs

of the barren, eggs of women
whose wombs split in childbirth.
Seamless eggs of a cracked future.
Shake them. Hear

their viscous potential.
If they are potatoes, let them be firm
and smooth as a hungry child's
swollen belly. Weigh them

in your palm: the heft of pestilence
inversely proportional
to the buoyancy of gluttony.
If they be stone, Lord,

let them be porous, so tears
may flow right through them.
Dense, heavy moons.
Tiny, stillborn moons.

AT A DISTANCE

She held her daughter as she would
a bird, as one who feels she hasn't earned
the right to care for such a creature,
starved of breath as she was on her way
from womb to world. And, after twelve years,
she holds her daughter still that way,
at a slight distance, as one would a prism,
turning her this way and that. Too close,
and she won't see from which direction
the light enters. How little she can do
to keep that light from escaping.

PIT

Pill in my mouth too tough
to chew, too bitter to swallow:
I suck the meat that clings
to it beyond compulsion.

There are days when I gnaw
at you, teeth bared and working
at some stubborn sinew
that won't part from its stone.

Be assured: if I did not love
you so, I'd have spat you
to the pavement, like a seed
not even fit for planting.

4

THUMBELINA'S MOTHER SPEAKS

~To Hans Christian Andersen

You can't rewrite the tale, it's too dispersed,
like wicked seed pods that, when touched, explode.
Each eager root another tuberous lie,
each thirsty leaf a gossip's waggling tongue.
No matter that the tale was hers—the bird
a mere translator of her partial truth.
Between your lines, another story breathes
and eats and shits and weeps its years away:
I learned to make a kind of life
without her. Hollow days I filled
with tending gardens, weaving willow strips
to keep my fingers occupied. You see,
we childless women have our ways of mothering.
My first rose bloomed today; it seemed to sing.

ASTHMA ATTACK

The bird in my throat
will not be still.

It squawks
behind the cage of my teeth,

wings incessant. For years,
I've lived with this flutter

that launches the rush
of spasms, gruff bird

that cannot be soothed.
Its feathers catch my words

mid-flight. The song of myself
falters, discordant.

Even after an attack
there is no silence,

only this damp wheeze,
wherein my life is sustained.

DIORAMA OF A GRAND FAILURE

Let two men inhabit the cardboard box
with their paper hands in their paper laps
on their paper chairs with the paper clock
a silent nod to the fallacy of time.

Let fake breaths ricochet from wall to ceiling
to stir the heads of our creations—
though there should be a formality to the chat
conducted within the box.

It may be appropriate for one or both parties
to be constrained by a mutual distrust or love,
which binds them like the bead of glue that affixes
the two-dimensional door to the inside of this box.

Let the wives be off building fairy tales with children
young enough to be graced by the bliss of ignorance.
Bless this diorama of a grand failure.

If there is a story behind the scene, free our men
from this artifice, prevent another chapter
from being written in the book
that would have contained both their lives.

If there were sense enough, stay the hand
that wields the scissors; add no more
to this dismal effect of thwarted domesticity.

Burn the paper before it divides our scene
into easts and wests of doubt.
Dry up the indelible markers that quiver
just inside the lines and never stray beyond.

JUST SO

My child, my child,
how could I let you go?

Those times I'd hurl you at the wall—
you, child I couldn't have, surrogate child,
child without piss or blood,
child my undeveloped breasts couldn't nourish.
You'd fix your glassy eyes on me and, then,
how could I give you up?

And now, I breach the mustiness
of this superfluous room
to brush your matted hair,
adjust your precisely bent arm
up to wave goodbye before I close the door
on you and your dozen positioned sisters
forever waving from the shelf
of a world I built just for you.

What am I
to perch you there, forget you,
return when I remember—
to adjust your hair the way,
sometimes, as I tend the azaleas,
a sudden breeze
resets the collar of my blouse
just so?

MY MOTHER'S TONGUE

My mother's tongue is burning
and, finally, she is not afraid
                     to tell us.

My tongue is on fire, she says.
To us, to the doctor, to the
                     oral specialist.

The doctors say *Rinse with this,*
and do not listen. *Idiopathic,*
                     they say.

My mother's tongue is burning.
Vocabulary as tinder. Her mouth
                     a matchbox.

She rinses with their chemicals
but the forest in her mouth
                     still smolders.

It isn't helping, she says. *I have to see
someone else.* What she means
                     is this:

*I have to tell someone who will
listen.* My mother's tongue
                     is burning

after years without complaint. It burns,
and, finally, she is not afraid
                     to speak.

NATURE CENTER

The bat is so small and the docent says that's
what people mention first when they see it.
And she is talking and my daughter is talking,
pulling me away to play with the insect puppets
and it's obvious the woman at the nature center
has so much knowledge to share and I, who have
still so much to learn, want her to keep talking
so I mention something about bats flying into people's hair
and then she's off again talking about what a misconception
that is because bats have such finely-tuned sonar
they would never do something as fool as that.
But *Mommy Mommy Mommy* breaks in and I
tear myself away from that bat, spread and pinned,
preserved beneath its glass, and I'm shoving my hand
into the fabric form of a spider, but I don't have enough
fingers on one hand to fill all the legs so three of them
flop as I scuttle it over to the puppet bird nest.
And still I hear the woman at the nature center
talking to us because she has so much to share
and we are the only ones there to hear and I,
I have such a need to absorb anything I can
that doesn't involve pink ponies or strawberry-
scented gel pens. She can see my skull split
open to receive her message. My eyes search out
the exhibits. The snake. I am reading wall text
out of the corner of my eye and feeding my hand
into another puppet as *Mommy Mommy Mommy*
distracts me before I can find out how long
the corn snake will be when it reaches maturity.

OYSTER SHELLS

The oyster knows how to keep
a secret, parting its lips
only when boiled alive.

Inflamed by Hypatia's devotion
to the truth, Cyril and his fanatics
stripped her naked in a church,

scraped the sticky truth of her flesh
from its bones with oyster shells.
They set Hypatia's still-writhing limbs

on the pyre. Her heresy
left to smolder, the acrid cause
of rationalism dispersed

like so much enlightened smoke
throughout a world
that refused to hold its breath.

BATH

Beneath my hands, her hair—an angelfine tangle in the water.

Every latent threat conjured in the gentle sway of that silken mass—a beautiful creature itself seemingly independent of its four-year-old skull.

Above her submerged form my breath catches until her eyes open and she grins and says *My ears are underwater. Say something to me.* I begin, *Once upon a time…*

By the way she closes her eyes and smiles, unresponsive, I know she cannot hear me.

A MATTER OF PRINCIPLE

I'd never made anything involving a ham hock before,
thought of it as a mere flavoring for Sunday's Cajun bean soup.

But after spooning the last of the soup for Tuesday's dinner,
as I carried the hock on a ladle toward the waste bin,

I noticed the meat, woven between the bone
and layers of fat, thick as a woolen sock, encasing it.

With a fork, I peeled away the outer layer, glimpsed
the yield awaiting me. This would be no delicate work.

I sunk my fingers in, pinching among gristle and bone
dislodging ruby chunks of the briny meat, scraping here

and there to ensure the morsels would be as lean as possible.
No waste but fat, a sheen on my fingers, viscous under my nails.

I thought of those who'd relish even what I rejected.
It was a matter of principle: peel and dig, scrape and sort,

the insubstantial sinew prized, a gem to gild our common plates.
With so many who'd take the parts fit only for rendering,

I owed it to them to get all I could from this chunk of meat I knew
would be so unhealthy for me. Damn the hypertension and cholesterol,

I would not let this become another regret to haunt me.
What else have I wasted?

SEAMSTRESS

She pulls the thread gently
along the seam of chiffon,

realizes she's stitching clouds
together again, realizes

the pricking of the needle
has opened a rift in the sky,

and memories move deftly
in and out of the fabric.

At last, the movement
becomes the memory

as the pattern, already laid out,
takes its shape in the cloth,

and she sees the future,
a glint of light projected

in the incessant steel of her
strobe-like and fleeting needle.

ADVICE TO MY DAUGHTER REGARDING HOUSES IN THE WOODS

One door to every house in the woods
is unlocked. And you are always so tired
that you try every entrance.

The beds are either too hard, or too soft.
Eventually, wherever you lie when your eyes
close will feel cozy as a coffin.

Don't be surprised when you are awakened
by bears or dwarves or the rasp of branches
that carve the name of your prince

into the bark of your dreams. Sleep is the worm
in the bird's throat in the house in the woods.
The apples and candy tart

with their poisons. And if fortune should house you
in that cottage in the glen, don't open your door
to just anyone. Hide

your auntie's magic from every spying crow.
I may not be around to stay your finger
from the spindle, to loosen

the taut ribbons from the shell of your ribcage.
No girl should be expected to splay her tresses
on a pillow of ignorance,

no matter how soft. That's why I'm telling you this
now. There will be beckoning fingers, kindly
strangers. Chimneys blowing their sweet

odors to draw you in as the mouse is drawn
to the cheese-baited trap. But, love, when you are finally
secured away by your prince

in the cold stone of his castle, may your tongue
recall the sweet warmth of the milky porridge
on which you once feasted.

The remembered kiss of the sparrow's foot
alighting on your palm, like a rune you rub
until the pads of your fingers are numb.

About the Author

BERNADETTE GEYER is the author of the chapbook *What Remains*, and recipient of a Strauss Fellowship from the Arts Council of Fairfax County. Her poems have appeared in *Oxford American, North American Review, The Midwest Quarterly, Verse Daily,* and elsewhere. Geyer is an instructor at The Writer's Center in Bethesda, Maryland, and teaches poetry to elementary school students through a program sponsored by the Arlington Cultural Affairs Department and the Arlington Public School Humanities Project.

About the Cover Artist

KATHLEEN KENDALL is an artist and art teacher living in northern Virginia. She studied at the University of West Florida, and received an MIS from Virginia Commonwealth University. Much of the imagery in her work is inspired by classical myths and legends that run across time and cultures, exploring personal mythic stories using symbolic imagery. Her work is primarily exhibited at Lorton Arts Foundation in Lorton, Virginia, online at Fine Arts America, and at kathleenkendall.com.

About the Hilary Tham Capital Collection

THE HILARY THAM CAPITAL COLLECTION (HTCC) is an imprint of The Word Works featuring juried selections from poets who volunteer to assist The Word Works in its mission to promote contemporary poetry. Judge Cornelius Eady selected the 2012 HTCC book.

In 1989, Hilary Tham was the first author published in the Capital Collection imprint. In 1994, when she became Word Works Editor-in-Chief, she revitalized and expanded the imprint. Tham died in 2005 and the imprint was renamed in her honor.

FROM THE HILARY THAM CAPITAL COLLECTION

    Mel Belin, *Flesh That Was Chrysalis,* 1999
    Doris Brody, *Judging the Distance,* 2001
    Sarah Browning, *Whiskey in the Garden of Eden,* 2007, 2nd printing 2011
    Grace Cavalieri, *Pine Crest Rest Home,* 1998
    Christopher Conlon, *Gilbert and Garbo in Love,* 2003, and
              Mary Falls: Requiem for Mrs. Surratt, 2007
    Donna Denizé, *Broken Like Job,* 2005
    W. Perry Epes, *Nothing Happened,* 2010
    James Hopkins, *Eight Pale Women,* 2003
    Brandon Johnson, *Love's Skin,* 2006
    Marilyn McCabe, *Motion Studies,* 2012
    Judith McCombs, *The Habit of Fire,* 2005
    James McEwen, *Snake Country,* 1990
    Miles David Moore, *The Bears of Paris,* 1995, and *Rollercoaster,* 2004
    Kathi Morrison-Taylor, *By the Nest,* 2008
    Michael Schaffner, *The Good Opinion of Squirrels,* 1996
    Maria Terrone, *The Bodies We Were Loaned,* 2002
    Hilary Tham, *Bad Names for Women,* 1989, and *Counting,* 2000
    Barbara Ungar, *Charlotte Brontë, You Ruined My Life,* 2011
    Jonathan Vaile, *Blue Cowboy,* 2005
    Rosemary Winslow, *Green Bodies,* 2007
    Michele Wolf, *Immersion,* 2011

The Word Works thanks the David G. Taft Foundation, Miles David Moore, and anonymous contributors for generous financial support of the Hilary Tham Capital Collection.

About The Word Works

The Word Works, a nonprofit literary organization, publishes contemporary poetry and presents public programs. Since 1981, it has sponsored the Washington prize, a monetary award to and book publication for an American or Canadian poet. Monthly, The Word Works offers free literary programs in the Chevy Chase, MD, Café Muse series, and each summer, it holds free poetry programs in Washington, DC's Rock Creek Park. Annually in June, two high school students debut in the Miller Poetry Series as winners of the Jacklyn Potter Young Poets Competition.

Since 1974, Word Works programs have included: "In the Shadow of the Capitol," a symposium and archival project on the African American intellectual community in segregated Washington, DC; the Gunston Arts Center Poetry Series (e.g. Ai, Carolyn Forché, and Stanley Kunitz); the Poet Editor panel discussions at The Writer's Center (e.g. John Hollander, Maurice English, Anthony Hecht, Josephine Jacobsen); and Master Class workshops (e.g. Agha Shahid Ali, Thomas Lux, Marilyn Nelson).

As a 501(c)3 organization, The Word Works has received awards from the National Endowment for the Arts, National Endowment for the Humanities, DC Commission on the Arts & Humanities, Witter Bynner Foundation, Poets & Writers, The Writer's Center, Bell Atlantic, the David G. Taft Foundation, and others, including many generous private patrons. The Word Works has established an archive of artistic and administrative materials in the Washington Writing archive housed in the George Washington University Gelman Library. The Word Works is a member of the Council of Literary Magazines and Presses and distributed by Small Press Distribution.

More information at WordWorksBooks.org

Other Word Works Books

Washington Prize Winners

Nathalie F. Anderson, *Following Fred Astaire*, 1998
Michael Atkinson, *One Hundred Children Waiting for a Train*, 2001
Carrie Bennett, *biography of water*, 2004
Peter Blair, *Last Heat*, 1999
Richard Carr, *Ace*, 2008
B.K. Fisher, *St. Rage's Vault*, 2012
Ann Rae Jonas, *A Diamond Is Hard But Not Tough*, 1997
Frannie Lindsay, *Mayweed*, 2009
Richard Lyons, *Fleur Carnivore*, 2005
Fred Marchant, *Tipping Point*, 1993, 3rd printing 1999
Ron Mohring, *Survivable World*, 2003
Brad Richard, *Motion Studies*, 2010
Jay Rogoff, *The Cutoff*, 1994
Prartho Sereno, *Call from Paris*, 2007
Enid Shomer, *Stalking the Florida Panther*, 1987, 2nd printing 1993
John Surowiecki, *The Hat City after Men Stopped Wearing Hats*, 2006
Miles Waggener, *Phoenix Suites*, 2002
Mike White, *How to Make a Bird with Two Hands*, 2011
Nancy White, *Sun, Moon, Salt*, 1992, 2nd edition 2010

International Editions

Yoko Danno & James C. Hopkins, *The Blue Door*
Moshe Dor (Barbara Goldberg, trans.), *Scorched by the Sun*
Moshe Dor, Barbara Goldberg, Giora Leshem, eds., *The Stones Remember*
Myong-Hee Kim, *Crow's Eye View: The Infamy of Lee Sang, Korean Poet*
Vladimir Levchev, *Black Book of the Endangered Species*

ADDITIONAL TITLES

    Karren L. Alenier, *Wandering on the Outside*

    Karren L. Alenier, Hilary Tham, Miles David Moore, eds.,
        Winners: A Retrospective of the Washington Prize

    Christopher Bursk, ed., *Cool Fire*

    Barbara Goldberg, *Berta Broadfoot and Pepin the Short*

    Jacklyn Potter, Dwaine Rieves, Gary Stein, eds.,
        Cabin Fever: Poets at Joaquin Miller's Cabin

    Robert Sargent, *Aspects of a Southern Story*
        A Woman From Memphis

www.ingramcontent.com/pod-product-compliance
Lightning Source LLC
Chambersburg PA
CBHW051704090426
42736CB00013B/2537